Eat Less and Move More: My Journey

By

Paul G. Brodie

Eat Less and Move More: My Journey

Copyright @ 2015 by Paul G. Brodie

Editing by Devin Rene Hacker

Published in the United States by BrodieEDU Publishing, 2015.

Disclaimer

The following viewpoints in this book are those of Paul Brodie. These views are based on his personal experience over the past forty years on the planet Earth, especially while living in the great state of Texas.

The intention of this book is to share his stories of struggles with weight and what has worked for *him* through his journey. It is highly recommended that you consult with your doctor prior to any weight loss plan and potential lifestyle change.

The views expressed are based on his personal experiences within the corporate world, education, and everyday life.

This book is dedicated to my mom, Barbara "Mama" Brodie. Without her support and motivation (and incredible cooking) I would literally not be here today.

I am also dedicating this book to everyone who has had struggles in life, especially with weight. Our greatest battle will always be against ourselves and winning that battle will be our greatest victory.

Contents

Foreword

Recently, I lost over 30 pounds. I feel dramatically different. It is crazy how one simple thing can impact your life.

I remember the feeling of being overweight. I was exhausted all the time. I wasn't very happy. I did not feel like doing anything. I did not feel like me.

Now, I am in the best shape of my life. I feel amazing. Naturally, everything in my outside world is matching my frequency inside.

Business is better. Breathing feels light like a feather. It used to feel heavy like a thick fog. I remember trying to force myself to do work related things. It was brutal. Now it's simple. Work is enjoyable. We all like doing things that are enjoyable.

If you want to be successful in life, it starts with your health. Your mind is a part of your body. Treat your body well and your mind will take care of itself. It's beautiful and will give you a chuckle when you see the simplicity of it.

As Buddha once said, "To keep the body in good health is a duty...otherwise we shall not be able to keep our mind strong and clear."

Paul Brodie's book teaches you how to do just this. He explains how to effectively go through the path of bettering your health and success.

Paul teaches you the one simple thing. He is able to do this because he, himself has gone through the process and effectively came out better on the other side. The one simple thing is figuring out how to effectively better your health and success every single day, consistently.

To learn how to implement this in your own life, I highly recommend reading through these pages more than once. The value is underneath the writing or as some would say…within it.

To your health and success,

Tyler Benjamin Wagner
Founder at Authorsunite.com
Bestselling Author of Conference Crushing

Introduction

I want to thank you for investing your time in reading my first book. This book is my four year journey to Eat Less and Move More that began in May 2011. I also want to be clear this is the first of two books about weight struggles. The process is far from over. I have lost weight and have finally gotten control of my weight issues, but I have a long way to go before I hit my final goal. In my view, our greatest battle in life will always be against ourselves and whether it is weight or other issues, it is always going to be an internal battle of you against yourself.

On May 2, 2011, I was 336 pounds, borderline type 2 diabetic, and recently recovered from both bronchitis and pneumonia. I actually felt like I was dying. As you can imagine, my health was not in the best shape.

In addition to my health, I also had major issues with stress as my ESL (English as a Second Language) program at school was getting shut down and that influenced my decision to leave. Not knowing where my next teaching position would be created a lot of stress. I was emotionally hurt by my program getting phased out, especially with the success my program had as one of the top ranked programs in the district for academic performance.

This combination of illness and stress affected my ability to sleep soundly or sometimes at all. I started to have heart palpitations, which was terrifying to say the least. I knew something was wrong. I scheduled an appointment with my doctor for Monday May 2, 2011. That day was rough. I could barely move, but I was determined to teach my ESL classes that day. I had been battling bronchitis and pneumonia since early March and I was determined to finish the school year strong for my kids. In the midst of all my health concerns, I was informed that all of my students in eighth grade scored Advanced or Advanced High on the TELPAS writing. This was a huge deal! Such great results that hadn't been achieved before!

My kids were already upset knowing that the program was coming to an end, but I made it clear that we would finish the year on a great note, by celebrating the past two years we had together. I managed to make it through the school day and went straight to the doctor's office once school was over. The doctor's visit did not go well. I was a borderline type 2 diabetic, my weight was out of control, my stress level was way too high, and if I continued the same path then I probably would not be around within the next 5-10 years. To say this was my wakeup call would be an understatement.

On the bright side, my doctor explained that due to my high weight, I should be able to take off a significant amount of weight by changing my lifestyle and reducing my calories to 2500 per day. I'm six foot three, big boned and have broad shoulders, all which help with carrying all of that weight. The 2500 calories would still give me plenty of food, but I would need to limit sugars and eventually change my lifestyle. I was very determined to change my life for the better and did a lot of research about what I could do to lose the weight and keep it off.

The first thing I did that day was to create an account on MyFitnessPal. I used the site to track everything that I ate and drank. It was a tedious process at first, but I got used to it and tracking calories became a part of my daily routine. They have a website in addition to the app, so you can use it wherever you go. With reducing my calories to 2500 a day and tracking each calorie through MyFitnessPal, I was ready to start the journey!

In this book I will share with you what I did to lose over sixty seven pounds, and more importantly keep most of the weight off. As of June 5, 2015 I'm still down forty nine of those sixty seven pounds originally lost. I will reveal both my successes and mistakes experienced through twenty plus years of fluctuating weight, while incorporating my life journey and my career in education as it all connects.

One of the main things I have found to be true as an educator is that we must learn from history. My history with food is extensive. I'll discuss my struggles with food, which I have had my entire life and will most likely continue to have.

My hope is that my story helps. My philosophy in anything I do, whether it is teaching, giving motivational seminars, or writing is to have the power of one. The power of one is my goal to help at least one person. I hope that person is you.

Chapter 1 School Days

Throughout my life my weight has gone up and down. I have lost over forty pounds on two previous occasions and ended up putting all of the weight back on. The first time this occurred was in 1991. I was 268 pounds at the age of 16 and had started marching band that August before high school. During the summer of 1991 I sat around the house drinking at least five to six cans of Dr. Pepper in addition to eating all sorts of unhealthy food. In other words, I acted like a typical teenager on summer vacation. In June I was weighing in around 250 pounds. Sitting around drinking soft drinks while eating tons of unhealthy food was a bad combination for both my heath and weight gain.

High school can be a brutal place. I knew that I needed to lose the weight for both health and social reasons. I changed my diet to eating only chicken and salads and over four months I went from 268 to 215 pounds. I kept off most of the weight for several years. I switched to Diet Coke that summer and have not had a Dr. Pepper since. Taking part in marching band during my high school years was a great way to keep off most of the weight. I was constantly going from 6:30 am until 9:00 pm with school, band and choir, and work. By the start of my senior year I was around 230 pounds. Unfortunately, the last semester of my senior year didn't involve marching band or choir and without that structure I ended up around 245 pounds by graduation.

After high school was over, college offered a lot of freedom and once I entered college, I gained the freshmen thirty. Without the structure of high school, I became lazy and had too much downtime. During most of that downtime, I hung out with friends while eating foods that I should never have eaten.

The second time that I lost weight I went from 288 to 236 pounds. The year was 1999 and I was 24 years old. This time I had done it by reducing my portions (no salads), but still drank Diet Cokes at least four to five times a day. I had gotten a gym membership and spent an hour a day, three days a week from March through December, splitting my time between cardio on the treadmill, weight training with free weights, and circuit training.

Within four years I put all of the weight back on and added an additional twenty pounds. This brought my total weight to 308 pounds. My main mistake was the college life. I pledged a social fraternity in 2000 and quickly got used to late night socializing which then meant stopping by fast food restaurants at 3:00 am to get burgers and fries. This wasn't exactly the best plan for dieting. Since I did not finish the pledging process I decided that I would consider joining another fraternity, but one that was a little more focused on academics and not just on socializing.

In 2001, I left college for a year in order to complete credits from a junior college. This was done to both save money and to become more focused. At this point I was working full time and going to school part time. I realized that I was spending way too much time socializing and I needed to get my life in order. Over the next year, I was able to complete some of my most difficult classes (algebra and accounting) and also keep my weight from getting worse. In fall 2002, I returned to my college at The University of Texas at Arlington. I was refreshed, focused, and ready to get my degree within the next two years. I was around 290 pounds and did not gain much weight over the past year. That fall I joined a business fraternity, Delta Sigma Pi (DSP) and loved it. I was able to spend time with a great group of people and also had a good balance of academics while still having fun. However, I did get back into the late night socializing and my weight did increase yet again over the next two years. By graduation in the fall of 2004, I was around 310 pounds.

During graduation I received a curveball that I did not pass my Operations Management class. That semester I had taken eighteen hours on three campuses and I definitely overextended myself. I was allowed to still walk and attend graduation. The only thing was that I would need to take the class again during maymester (three week period between the end of the spring semester and summer school). I was devastated by the news, but still had an amazing graduation. I knew that I would get through the class in May, which I did. My weight in 2005 continued to stay around 310 as I was not doing as much late night socializing now that college was wrapping up.

From 1992 to 2005 I worked for a market research company. I was able to work my way through college and received several promotions. Once I finally officially graduated in May 2005 I had zero college debt, but I did receive another curveball. The market research company that I had worked for since 1992 was bought out. I was given a great severance package and was grateful for the opportunity to work at a wonderful company that taught me a lot. The only problem was that I was a college graduate without a job.

Chapter 2: Corporate World

I was hired in August 2005 as a Management Trainee at Enterprise Rent-A-Car. On Labor Day Weekend 2005 I was swimming in my pool on that Sunday and suddenly felt really sick. I decided to go to bed at 5:00 pm that night and slept until late the following morning. I was also really cold, which was strange as I am usually warm. I checked my temperature that morning and had a 102 degree fever. As I was feeling extremely dizzy, my mom drove me to my doctor's office. I was diagnosed with a Urinary Tract Infection and was also told that I had issues with my kidneys. I was strongly advised to give up carbonated beverages and to mainly drink water and tea. This was my first wakeup call at thirty years old.

My love of Diet Cokes goes back many years. I would probably drink sixty to eighty ounces a day from 1991 to 2005. I loved the taste and was convinced that the caffeine motivated me though the work and school day. I would always have extra Diet Coke cans in my backpack to ensure that I would have plenty of caffeine to make it through the day.

When I started at Enterprise that August, the first thing I put in my backpack were three Diet Cokes.

The doctor was telling me to give up one of the things that I felt was impossible to make it through the day without. My choice was simple, give up carbonated drinks (soft drinks, beer) and get healthy or continue to drink soft drinks and stay sick.

I never thought that I could give up Diet Coke, but I did. Since 2005 I have not had one Diet Coke, nor do I miss it. The first couple of weeks were rough. I did get headaches because my body was used to the caffeine. I increased my water intake and drank hot earl gray tea. It took around six months to fully recover, but my body did eventually get better.

I was moving around a lot with Enterprise as a Management Trainee and had a lot of success with making elite for insurance sales on a monthly basis. I was even recognized as a top three performer out of over one hundred and fifty Management Trainees throughout the Dallas Fort Worth Metroplex. Within eight months I received a promotion to Management Assistant and a few months later became an Assistant Manager. The only problem was that we ate a lot of bad food as we rushed around throughout the day. The days went quickly, but so did lunch. Usually we only had a few minutes to run to get lunch so fast food was often our only option. This was not the best decision health wise because I could have lost a significant amount of weight if I would have chosen to eat right.

In 2007, I was employed by a nurse recruiting company. It meant less hours at work and much more money. I resigned from Enterprise, but was grateful for having had the opportunity to learn a great deal about sales and customer service. Enterprise is one of the best companies to start a career with after college. It will always be an experience that I look back on fondly. In hindsight, leaving for the job in nurse recruiting was one of the best decisions that I have ever made as it helped me find my true calling.

For the next six months I was sitting in a cubicle with a headpiece attached to my ears. The job was pretty easy and I was promoted to an Account Manager within three months. Unfortunately, I was sitting for the entire day and not moving around much. The weight increased and I was feeling weak. I decided that I would need to eat a little healthier now that I was sitting all day. I ended up losing some weight and was probably around the 300 pound mark by August.

I ate eat snacks throughout the day. Although, I would have probably lost more weight if some of my snacks were not Pringles potato chips and Gatorade. I did have some of those 100 calorie snack packs, which helped with the hunger that appeared working long hours and irregular schedules. The company would bring in pizza on Wednesday's, but I would eat my own food instead, which usually was a sandwich. As the months progressed, I realized that I needed a career change. The corporate world was no longer for me.

Chapter 3 Leap Of Faith

In October 2007, I decided that I had enough. This was not the correct career direction I wanted anymore. I took a huge leap of faith and left my job. At the time I was very careful with my money and had built up a significant reserve. My job had paid very well, but I also knew that there was more to life than just sitting in a cubicle recruiting nurses.

My weight increased a little with being off work, but it was the best decision I have ever made. Over the next several months I wrote out multiple lists about where my next step would be. Money was not that important. As long as I had enough to pay the mortgage and bills with a little left over at the end of the month, I knew I would be fine. I was more concerned with having the opportunity to help others again. At Enterprise I was able to help out a lot of up and coming employees by serving as a mentor in the mentoring program and training employees, which I loved doing.

I wanted to have a position which would give me a little more time off. For the past several years I had worked anywhere between 45-60 hours per week, only getting one to two weeks off per year. Work life balance would have to be a huge factor in my next career step. I also wanted a position where I would be moving around, to support my healthy lifestyle. What I realized is that everything that I desired was in the realm of education.

Mr. Brodie, Teacher. I had to think long and hard about that title. Could Paul Brodie, class clown, rebel, smart, but stubborn student, teach other students? I thought back to my time as a student and I remembered Mr. Sangalli. My awesome US History teacher (and current Facebook friend) that I had my junior year at James Bowie High School. He was a new teacher and a really cool guy. Mr. Sangalli was fair with the students, had great lectures, and cared greatly about his kids.

I remembered one class in particular in 1993. It was after the Dallas Cowboys won the Super Bowl, which was a huge deal at not only our school, but all over Texas. There was a parade to celebrate the Super Bowl in Dallas that happened on the previous day, which several of the students in class went to. They took the day off from school with their parents' permission (at least that's what they said) and went to the parade. Unfortunately, there were some problems at the parade and several kids had some issues with the police. That day in class, one of the students brought up what had happened at the parade with the police. Several of the kids in class who went to the parade were African American and felt they were targeted by the police. Mr. Sangalli spent the rest of the class talking about race relations. I was amazed because just about any other teacher would have changed the subject and went on with the lesson. Instead, Mr. Sangalli had an open and fair discussion with the entire class about race relations. Not only for the rest of that class period, but also for part of the next day's lesson.

I decided that I wanted to have the same effect that Mr. Sangalli had on his kids. In January 2008, I started the process of becoming a teacher. There were several tests that I would need to take. I was also eligible to start substitute teaching. My weight at the time was probably around 320 pounds. After the Christmas Holiday I would typically gain 5-10 pounds through enjoying the season.

On February 14, 2008, I started my first day as a substitute teacher. I accepted an assignment to teach choir at a Junior High School in Arlington, TX, the same school district that I attended. What I would realize in the first fifteen minutes, is that this was either a horrible mistake or the greatest decision of my life. No pressure!

What could go wrong? Why wouldn't you want to spend a day teaching teenagers on Valentine's Day? Combining mainly female students with heightened emotions and hormones, chocolate, and Valentine's Day? Actually, the day went well and I ended up falling in love with teaching within a few minutes of starting. I realized this was what I wanted to do in life and immediately continued the process of getting certified as a teacher.

Over the next several months, I continued to substitute teach at many schools in Arlington including several schools that I went to as a kid. Sadly, all of the teachers that taught me were gone for the most part. However, one teacher at James Bowie High School still remained.

I accepted a teaching assignment for a World History class in April at Bowie. I decided to check out my old school and found that Mr. Sangalli was still teaching. After school, I stopped by his room and introduced myself and he remembered me immediately. I told him he had a great impact in me wanting to become a teacher and he mentioned that he needed a substitute teacher for the following week. I immediately accepted his offer and was able to serve as his replacement for two awesome days. It is amazing how things come full circle in life and it was a great honor to serve as a substitute for someone who helped inspire me to enter teaching.

Over the summer, I went through alternative teaching certification and went to several job fairs. I found out from one of the coordinators in Arlington ISD about an ESL position that was opening up. Within a week I interviewed and received a job offer to teach ESL full time.

Chapter 4 Teacher Man

In August 2008, I had accomplished my goal. I was officially a teacher. Nothing can prepare you for life as a teacher. I learned very quickly that I had a lot to learn about classroom management and lesson planning. Fortunately, I had an amazing principal and an instructional facilitator that both helped greatly in my development as a teacher. Within a few months, I was nominated for teacher of the month. By the 2010-2011 school year I was a finalist for teacher of the year.

During this time in 2008 my weight was around the 315-320 range. One of the drawbacks about having the time off during the previous nine months was that I was at home a lot and did not move around as much as I wanted to. I spent a lot of time researching teaching and related careers while studying for the multiple tests and certifications that I would need to take.

During the spring 2009, semester I was presented with an amazing opportunity. What I have learned in life is that when great opportunities come along, you must take them. The alternative certification program that I completed during summer 2008 had a partnership with Louisiana College in Pineville, Louisiana. The partnership was just starting and was open to all alumni of the teaching certification program. We were offered the opportunity to get our Master of Arts in Teaching within two years and would also receive eighteen hours of credit through our certification and teacher experience from our role in the classroom. It would only cost $5000.00 for grad school due to the program being brand new. I knew this was an amazing opportunity and I entered the program in the spring of 2009. This was done in addition to being a first year teacher, but I knew that I would be better because of it.

I took on another challenge that year as well. I remained involved in the business fraternity that I was inducted into at UT Arlington. After graduation, a group of recent alumnus formed our DSP alumni chapter in Arlington. Since becoming an alumnus in 2005, I served in many volunteer positions and was the president of the alumni chapter for several years. In 2009 I decided that I wanted to run again. This time for a national position on the Board of Directors for Delta Sigma Pi Business Fraternity. I was in a contested election and had the great opportunity of giving a ten minute speech in front of the entire delegation during the national convention (Washington DC

Grand Chapter Congress). I was elected as a National Vice President.

Between those three things my life was very busy. I also began giving more motivational seminars as I officially debuted my PMA: Positive Mental Attitude seminar in Boston, MA in fall 2008. In addition, I was also giving seminars at campuses throughout Texas. The PMA seminar shared stories of my philosophy on the power of being positive and my journey through the corporate world, as well as going into education.

One of the biggest mistakes I made during this time was not keeping track of my weight. I let my busy life be my excuse. What was even more disturbing, was that I was regularly buying clothes with waists ranging from 44-46 inches and shirts from three to four XL without a passing thought.

My life continued to be extremely busy in 2009 and 2010. Grad School was tough. Even though it was all online, it was just as difficult as getting a degree on campus. The work was challenging, but I loved it because it was all about teaching. I graduated with my Master of Arts Degree in Teaching in December 2010 with a 3.89 grade point average and finally saw the beautiful campus at Louisiana College for graduation.

After seeing my reflection in the graduation pictures a few days later, I realized that I was starting to look like a bloated version of myself. I had a goatee for many years and noticed that my goatee was getting larger and that I wasn't trimming it as much. My reasoning was because it would help cover the facial fatness (credit to Dave Glanzrock for the phrase).

Spring 2011 came around quickly. School was going great! I heard that the state budget cuts weren't going well (thank you Rick Perry), but that all efforts were being made to keep the ESL program due to the success that we were having. I was confident that the program would persist. In my mind, there was no way they could end such an excellent program. Lesson 27, logic and school districts do not always go together.

In late March I was told that my ESL program would not continue due to budget. To say I was upset would be an understatement. I decided that I wanted to continue to teach ESL so I decided to resign. It was a risk, but a risk worth taking. *The moment that we no longer take risks in life then we are no longer really living.*

Unfortunately, my leaving caused a lot of hurt with my kids. I always had (and continue to have) a very open and honest relationship with both my students and their parents. I told them about my resignation the day after it was submitted because I wanted them to hear it from me first. They were not happy to say the least. Several wanted to have a protest and I told them that it would not change anything. My eighth graders were all going to high school and many of them were eligible to exit the ESL program due to their successful progress. Roughly half of my seventh graders were also eligible to exit the program so I knew they would be alright.

Chapter 5 Beginning of the End

April was a stressful time, but the stress and illness started well before that. I started to have a head cold in late February. During that time I was teaching through the week and I traveled on the weekends for three straight weeks for my commitment as a National Vice President with DSP. The head cold started after the first weekend of travel to a leadership conference in Cleveland, OH. I took some over the counter medication and figured that it would get better. The next week, I traveled to San Francisco, CA for another leadership conference. I presented my PMA seminar at both conferences. During the weekend in San Francisco, I found out that I was going to be challenged for re-election for my National Vice President position by another board member. I love DSP greatly, but serving as a National Vice President was wearing me down both physically and emotionally. By this point, the politics on the Board of Directors were unbearable and I was actually considering not running again.

The combination of stress from both school and DSP was not good. I began to notice that I was gaining weight again and was pretty sure that I was at my highest weight. Once I got back from

San Francisco I had one more trip. I was not giving a seminar at the Myrtle Beach, SC leadership conference, but was scheduled to speak at Wingate University, NC. I had made it through the week teaching my classes and stubbornly got on that plane. I was flying to Charlotte, NC. My good friend was the DSP District Director at Wingate and he was going to drive us to Myrtle Beach the next day. I should never have gotten on that flight.

My throat began to close. I was choking and could barely breathe. Fortunately, I had upgraded my seat to first class so at least I could get water throughout the flight and be comfortable. Once I landed we went to Wingate University and I gave the seminar. Afterwards, I had several hot teas with some whiskey to help my throat. I started to feel a little better and we drove down to Myrtle Beach.

I continued to drink water throughout the day even as my throat continued to close. On that Saturday during the conference I continued to get sick. I had a meeting scheduled with most of my national committee that I was chair of and had to cut the meeting short because I could not stop sweating. At that point, I went back to my hotel room and slept for several hours. I made it back downstairs for the dinner banquet and dance. I had several friends check in on me and bringing me by orange juice and some Tylenol. After about an hour I went back to bed.

When I got back to Texas that Sunday night I decided that I would tough it out and make it through my classes on Monday. It was a rough day and I went to the doctor's office after school. My doctor diagnosed me with both bronchitis and pneumonia. He told me that it was very bad and had I have waited another day, I would have ended up in the hospital. I was given several breathing treatments and multiple prescriptions. Fortunately, spring break was coming up and I literally spent that entire week sleeping. The week off helped improve my health so I was able to teach my classes upon returning. At that point, I was still sick, but I could tough it out and make it through.

Chapter 6 Listen to Your Body

As you may have gathered by now, I tend to be a little stubborn. One of the greatest lessons I have learned over the past several years is to listen to my body. The past two chapters in particular have shown that life moves pretty fast. With my commitments I chose to tough it out and through my efforts ended up with both bronchitis and pneumonia.

I used to have the philosophy that I would sleep when I was dead. During my final semester at UT Arlington I was lucky to sleep a few hours a night with morning, afternoon, and evening classes across three campuses while working full time.

From 2009 to 2011 through my commitments with teaching, grad school, and as a board member in DSP, my time was very limited as was my sleep. I would spend many nights burning the midnight oil going to bed at 2:00 or 3:00 am and waking up at 7:30 am for school.

I was incredibly determined to keep my commitments and make every event and conference call. This is what caused me to get sick, by over extending myself. In hindsight, it was the best thing that could have happened though because it resulted in the wakeup call I received on May 2, 2011.

Chapter 7 Wakeup Call

May 2, 2011 changed my life for the better. That night I immediately created an account on MyFitnessPal and downloaded the app to my phone. I used the app daily and began to look up all foods that I ate. It was amazing how quickly calories added up and I instantly started to use the calories as a budget. Kind of how a National Basketball Association General Manager uses a salary cap. My salary cap was food and I was going to manage it to the best of my ability.

May 6, 2011 was another wakeup call. My doctor wanted to do some tests to make sure that my heart was alright. To be safe, I had my mom drive me since I was not sure how I would be after the test. The test involved me running on a treadmill for as long as possible with equipment monitoring my progress and heart rate. It did not go well.

After about six minutes on the treadmill I was worn out. I knew that I was out of shape, but did not realize how bad it was. The doctor stopped the test after six minutes because I literally could not run anymore. It was embarrassing. Not only because I was running with only shorts on, but also because of how large had my stomach become. That experience was something that I will never forget. The worst part was seeing how worried my mom was as I struggled to catch my breath.

Over the years I had seen my mom get worried about me, but this was different. She was terrified that I was not going to be around much longer because I was in such bad shape after running on the treadmill. Witnessing the fear in my mom's eyes further motivated me to make this lifestyle change.

On the bright side, my heart was fine. However, I was diagnosed with sleep apnea. It was suggested that I take chamomile tea at night before going to bed and begin taking melatonin. Regular exercise and stress reduction were the additional recommendations.

Chapter 8 Eat Less and Move More

My weight was down seven pounds from 335 to 328 pounds. The weight was coming off quickly due to the food adjustments I began making on that Monday night.

I bought a pedometer to track my steps daily. Immediately, I switched from sugary desserts to having fruit instead. I also switched from bread to whole grain wraps for lunches. Dinners featured grilled steak or chicken with a lot of green vegetables. I still had some cheats with one mint chocolate chip Klondike bar (240 calories) and one Cadbury's chocolate Easter egg (150 calories).

By the end of May I had lost 18 pounds, which brought me from 335 to 317 pounds. In June the school year ended and I moved all of my stuff out of my classroom. I knew that I would need to come up with a way to stay fit in the summer.

It wasn't long before I realized that I hated working out at a gym and I needed to find something to do at home. After doing some research, I decided that exercising in my pool was the way to go.

Working out in the pool would offer a lot of resistance as most of my body would be underwater. It would be easier on my joints than running or jogging around the neighborhood. Eating less would dictate most of my weight loss. However, moving more would be very important and I was thrilled to find a great way to stay in shape in the summer.

I started working out in my pool in mid-June. I would get in the pool and run and jog in place and move my arms throughout the workout. I worked out four days a week for 30-45 minutes burning on average 500-700 calories. I would do chin ups (three rounds of ten) on my diving board. Typically, I ran in place for thirty minutes, swam to the diving board to complete my chin ups and would swim back to the shallow end to run in place for three minutes and then swim back to the diving board for another round of chin ups. I would then do the same thing one more time.

One of the keys to a great workout is having the right music to motivate you. The first song that plays during a workout sets the tone and is critical to having a great start. My first song is always Gonna Fly Now from Rocky. Having the right songs for different parts of your workout is also critical. Below is my workout mix for 2011. Usually, I start to hit a wall around the twenty minute mark so I know that I have to have a great song for that time segment. My song to combat that wall was Till I Collapse by Eminem. I strongly encourage you to spend time coming up with the right mix for your workout.

Workout Mix Summer 2011

01 Rocky Theme (Gonna Fly Now)

02 Rocky IV Training Montage (Rocky training in Russia)

03 A View to a Kill by Duran Duran

04 Feel So Close by Calvin Harris

05 Let It Rock by Kevin Rudolf

06 Till I Collapse by Eminem

07 Amazing by Kayne West

08 Man in the Box by Alice In Chains

09 Head Sprung by LL Cool J

10 Sucker Punch Mashup I Want It All and We Will Rock You by Queen

I greatly increased my water intake and would drink between 150 to 200 ounces of water per day. Each morning I would get up and drink fifty ounces of water. On work out days I would get in the pool and work out and then drink another fifty ounces of water. I would have a side salad and then an open faced chicken or steak sandwich (wheat bread roll) with lots of peppers and onions with Heinz 57 BBQ sauce. For dinner I would have grilled chicken or steak with green vegetables. Dessert would be either a Klondike bar or a Cadbury's Easter egg in addition to thirty grapes and fifteen strawberries. I indulged in some minute maid light lemonade that I turned into popsicles. The popsicle was 1-5 calories each and were delicious. This more than stopped the sugar cravings.

Normally, I would go out for one cheat meal per week. This is something that I highly recommend. You MUST have a cheat meal at least once per week. It will make a big difference in how you feel and more importantly will satisfy a craving.

Through this process I learned how to manage my food in a variety of settings as my mom and I went on our annual family vacation in June. We went to Surfside, TX for the week to enjoy the beach. During the day I had whole grain wraps with lettuce, ham, cucumber, pickles, with honey mustard and also had those 100 calorie snack packs for dessert accompanied by strawberries and grapes.

For dinner each night there was a great grill (Pirate Grill) that we would get a burger with shrimp paella instead of fries and a beer. That week I managed to still lose two pounds by being careful about what I ate and by walking at the beach.

By the end of July 2011, I was under 300 pounds at 296 prior to leaving for Louisville, KY for the national convention (Louisville Grand Chapter Congress). Another great thing happened in July. I was called about an opening to run the Aspire After School Program for a middle school in the Birdville Independent School District. A few days later I interviewed for the position. This was a different direction than the one I had originally hoped to follow in order to continue teaching ESL. What I realized is that many ESL programs were getting phased out due to the theory that if the school districts required all teachers to become ESL certified that would have the same impact in the long run. It would also give me a break from the teaching in the classroom. <u>Lesson 27, logic and school districts do not always go together.</u>

I previously worked with the after school program in Arlington as a soccer coach at my junior high school during all three years that I taught. It appeared to be a different direction, but also a great new avenue. While I was in Louisville for Grand Chapter Congress I received the offer of employment to run the program and accepted. I would begin employment the day after I returned from Louisville.

Chapter 9 Polytricks

Louisville was an interesting experience. After serving for two years on the Board of Directors for DSP I was ready to get out. In hindsight, I should have withdrawn my name earlier that year and retired. DSP, like many other organizations, has great things and not so great things. The great thing is that many people love DSP and are very passionate. The not so great thing is that many people love DSP and are very passionate. Since 2009, I had a completely different perspective seeing things at the boardroom level. I witnessed things from several board members that I felt went completely against our philosophy. The political side could become very unpleasant, and the opposition in my re-election made sure of it.

I ended up not getting re-elected and honestly I took it as a blessing. While it was disappointing, it was one of the best things that could have happened to me. Ironically, by 2013, the position was eliminated at the Seattle Grand Chapter Congress Convention by a vote of the congress. I do not say that as a negative because quite frankly I supported eliminating the position as well. What I did realize is that, *no matter how hard you work*

and no matter how much you make a difference,
sometimes you just have to let things go.

I officially retired from the political side of DSP
after the election. The best part was that I had an
epic retirement party that night in my suite!
Throughout the evening almost two hundred
people attended. It was a great way to celebrate
the end of a chapter and the start of another.

I learned many lessons about polytricks during
those two years. It was a phrase a friend came up
with a few years ago (credit to Gilbert Landras)
and it perfectly sums up politics at all levels.

It was a great weight off my shoulders as that
same person who coined the phrase polytricks,
also gave me a great opportunity to serve as a
District Director for the chapter at The University
of Texas at Austin. He served as a Regional Vice
President in DSP and was needing to appoint a
District Director at UT Austin. A District Director
in DSP is someone who helps by giving advice
and support to a college chapter. They also make
sure the chapter is following the rules and staying
on point. I have had the honor to serve in that role
for the past four years and am officially retiring
from the position this year.

Chapter 10 Next Chapter in Education

I started work as an after school grant coordinator the day after I returned from Grand Chapter Congress. It would be different going from teaching in the classroom to serving in an administrative role, but I looked forward to the challenge. I was also looking forward to taking off more weight.

I was 296 pounds upon my return from Louisville. Within the next three months I went from 296 to 278. I brought my wraps for lunch and for the most part ate at home for dinner. The weight loss eventually started to take longer, but that was expected considering that I had lost almost sixty pounds in seven months.

Work was going well. I had a bit of a rough start getting everything down, but I was quickly getting things the way I wanted. I hired a great team of people to help in that process.

I survived the Christmas season and waited to weigh myself until February. My last weigh in being December 10, 2011 (276.2) and my next weigh in February 10 (275.8). I always do my weigh in as soon as I wake up in the morning and was very happy to see a weight loss, especially as the holidays almost always guarantee a weight gain. This is why I recommend not getting another weigh in post holidays until at least late January. That way you do not feel discouraged in case of a weight gain.

One of the things I did notice through the next several months was that my weight loss was getting very slow. I started to get frustrated with this. One thing change with my food was no longer eating at school during lunch. In hindsight I realized that this was a mistake.

I worked in Haltom City and they had some of the best Pho and Thai restaurants in Texas. One of my fellow grant coordinators had become a good friend and introduced me to several of these great restaurants, which I began to rotate between for lunch throughout the week. Looking back, the main issue was the amount of white rice I was eating with the entrees. It did give me a much needed break from being at school. I shared a computer lab with another teacher and we had large groups of fairly rowdy students in the room.

On March 28, 2012 I finally broke the 270 barrier and weighed in at 269.6. I was absolutely thrilled that after several frustrating months I was finally below 270. It felt like it took forever. This was the start of the downfall of my weight loss.

Over the next three months my lightest weight would be 268.5. While enjoying all of the great Asian food in Haltom City, I got hooked on sashimi (essentially cooked sushi). I would meet up with another grant coordinator at least 2-3 times a week during May and June to get sashimi. We became friends with the restaurant owner and he hooked us up with all you can eat sushi for twenty dollars including any soft drinks that we wanted.

I didn't drink any carbonated beverages with the exception of sprite on occasion. I would mix sprite with water (still do from time to time) as it definitely helped with the sashimi. What I later came to realize was that I NEVER should have eaten all of that white rice because it severely impeded my weight loss.

During summer of 2012 I was at the lightest weight that I have been in over a decade. I felt great about myself and thought that a little sashimi wouldn't bother my weight. I was wrong.

In late June, I weighed myself again and I was back over 270. I was very discouraged by this and at that point figured that I would just stay around the 270 mark. My thought process what that I was fitting comfortably into size 38 and 40 inch pants and I was wearing either XL or XXL clothes. I felt very comfortable with my progress and I thought that I should enjoy having some junk food again. I know what I am doing and there is no way that I will ever gain all of the weight back. This was not the best way of thinking.

As a grant employee we had to work more days. When I was a teacher we were on a 187 day contract and we would usually be off by the first week of June and would return in mid-August. As a grant employee we were on 236 day contracts and would work throughout summer. The nice part was being awarded an additional ten days of vacation days. This put our contract at roughly 226 as long as we used the days which I always did. We also ran a summer program that would cover most of June.

After June I only worked around 8-10 days in July to have some semblance of a summer break. Summer was when I would work out in the pool and improve my cardiovascular conditioning while burning some more weight. One of the great benefits to working out in the pool is that it's much easier on your bones and joints. Another great part about pool workouts is that running and jogging in place underwater offers a lot of resistance. You can easily burn five hundred calories within thirty minutes depending on the intensity that you are working out at.

Workout Mix Summer 2012

01 Rocky Theme (Gonna Fly Now)

02 Rocky IV Training Montage (Rocky training in Russia)

03 A View to a Kill by Duran Duran

04 Stronger by Kayne West

05 Cruel Summer by Bananarama

06 Till I Collapse by Eminem

07 Amazing by Kayne West

08 Rocky Going the Distance

09 Head Sprung by LL Cool J

10 Sucker Punch Mashup I Want It All and We Will Rock You by Queen

I would still workout two to three days a week, but there was something different with my food.

My cravings changed and instead of having a breakfast of eggs and ham, I wanted breakfast sandwiches instead. For some reason, I was having bread cravings again. I was bored with the wraps. Another huge mistake in hindsight.

One of the things I have discovered about my body is that white rice and breads make me bloat and I will not lose weight if I am eating those foods on a regular basis. Everyone's body is different. I have learned both of those foods are foods that I do not need to be eating often.

I stopped weighing myself and over the next year went from 270 to 281.3 (June 13, 2013). The weight was coming back on, yet my mentality was that my clothes still fit and I only put on a few pounds.

Summer was again upon us but I only worked out a few times in the pool. My workout mix was still there to motivate me when I did manage to exercise.

Workout Mix Summer 2013

01 Rocky Theme (Gonna Fly Now)

02 Rocky IV Training Montage (Rocky training in Russia)

03 A View to a Kill by Duran Duran

04 Rolling in Sweet Dreams mashup with Adele and Eurythmics

05 Lose Yourself to Dance by Daft Punk

06 Eye of the Tiger by Survivor

07 Amazing by Kayne West

08 Rocky Going the Distance

09 Sucker Punch Mashup I Want It All and We Will Rock You by Queen

10 We Own It by Wiz Khalifa

My weight seemed to stay pretty constant. I stopped weighing myself, which ended up not being good decision in the long run. Summer ended and the new school year was upon us. That fall I continued to go out to lunch, but was going to barbeque, burger, and breakfast restaurants in addition to eating Pho and Thai food. I nearly always felt terrible and bloated after eating that food for lunch. This is when things got worse.

Chapter 11 Weight Gain

By the end of 2013 I noticed that my clothes were getting tighter. Barely any of my XL clothes would fit and I continued to refuse to get on the scale. I decided that the scale was my enemy and that I would no longer waste my time with it. I now can see that this was fear presenting itself because I was terrified to see what number was on the scale. I was pretty sure that I was over the three hundred pound mark.

In February 2014 I was going to Chicago to present my new seminar Positivity Attracts. Prior to leaving for Chicago I was getting my clothes ready. I realized that it was going to be really cold in Chicago and I wanted to wear one of my DSP sweaters since it was a leadership conference for the fraternity. The sweater was a 3XL and I figured it would fit loosely, but that I could still wear it. When I tried it on it was not that loose.

The sweater fit quite well and I started to get worried. How much weight had I gained? I decided that I would need to change my eating habits again, but something else did not feel right. I was eating pretty well for the most part, yet the weight was up. I attributed it to my careless consumption over the holiday season in 2013. The weight gain was most likely at least ten pounds and deep down I knew that I was probably close to 310 pounds.

Over the next several months I ate better. I reduced my bread intake and I finally got bored eating out with all the barbeque, burgers, breakfast restaurants, Asian foods and specifically white rice. In the summer of 2014 I was back in the pool and working out again, although I only worked out a couple times a week. I was losing weight and figured that I was back under three hundred pounds. My mentality was that at least I only put on half the weight and not all of it. It was not a bad mentality at that time, but I knew that I needed to get back in shape.

Workout Mix Summer 2014

01 Rocky Theme (Gonna Fly Now)

02 Rocky IV Training Montage (Rocky training in Russia)

03 A View to a Kill by Duran Duran

04 Rolling in Sweet Dreams mashup with Adele and Eurythmics

05 Lose Yourself to Dance by Daft Punk

06 Eye of the Tiger by Survivor

07 Amazing by Kayne West

08 Rocky Going the Distance

09 Sucker Punch Mashup I Want It All and We Will Rock You by Queen

10 We Own It by Wiz Khalifa

I really liked the 2013 mix so for 2014 I left it as the same mix. It did the job but I probably should have added some new music to change things up.

Chapter 12 Back in the Classroom

After a great three years as a grant coordinator, I was ready for the next chapter of my teaching career. In my view, we had the best after school program in the school district. My principal also agreed with that assessment. With the grant ending I decided that it was time to return to the classroom.

In April 2014, I took the Special Education teacher certification. This would make me eligible to teach Special Education at all grade levels. This was my third teacher certification in addition to my 4-8 grade generalist certification (science, English, math, social studies) and also my ESL certification (English as a Second Language supplemental). There were not a lot of teacher openings that were posted in June and July, which made things a little stressful, especially with my grant officially ending on July 31, 2014.

It's funny how things work out in life. I found out about a Special Education opening for the Hurst-Euless-Bedford Independent School District. The position posted on July 30 and I immediately applied. I was called by the school district on August 1 and had an interview on August 5. Ironically, on August 4, I received a call from

Birdville ISD offering me the special education teaching position that I interviewed for back in Mid-July. I also received a call about another grant coordinator position that had just opened up. For some reason, I had a good feeling about the position in HEB and told Birdville that I had an interview coming up that was already scheduled and that I would need a couple of days to make my decision. It was not quite a decision on the level of LeBron James, but I wanted to make sure that I listen to all parties to decide where I wanted to take my talents (credit to LeBron James). Most importantly, I followed my gut and I know that I made the correct decision.

I interviewed with HEB on Tuesday morning August 5 and was offered the position that afternoon, which I accepted. Out of respect, I contacted the other interested parties and told them that I accepted the offer to teach in HEB and that I was grateful for the offers. It was time to return to the classroom.

My weight was getting under control again and I was eating clean for most of the summer. I was able to get in several pool workouts, but definitely could have worked out more. However, my clothes were looser and I figured I was down at least ten pounds since January.

Chapter 13 Teaching is Like Riding a Bike

I was a little hesitant about returning to the classroom. Would I still have it? Could I teach Special Education students? The answer to those questions was a resounding yes.

I started teacher training with HEB on Wednesday August 6 as they have training for new teachers to the school district. The training was great even if it did end summer a little earlier than expected. I was thrilled to be teaching again!

Once the two weeks of training was over it was time to start the school year. Teachers typically have to report back within a week to week and a half prior to the students returning for the new school year. I had a roughly one week to get my classroom ready and to also find out which subjects I would be teaching.

My classroom was a mess. It was an old portable and was apparently used as a storage room for the summer. It took many hours of blood, sweat, and tears, but I finally got the room ready to go for the new school year. I also found out that I would be teaching four units of science, one unit of English, and one unit of social skills.

The school year started in late August and I was raring to go. I immediately bonded with my kids. They were special ed and several had severe learning disabilities. Regardless, one thing that I have learned over the years is that kids are kids.

I spent the next month game planning for the rest of the school year, quickly becoming a science expert. I aligned the lessons with the goals and objectives (TEKS) for their learning and upcoming standardized testing.

My weight at this point I felt was down at least 5-10 pounds. The only problem was that I was not sure how much weight I had put on because I still hated that scale. I was burning at least 700-800 calories through tracking my pedometer, but I was eating foods that I shouldn't... again. This time it was pizza. I was eating pizza at least two times per week, with the mentality that I needed a reward for my hard work at school. This was another mistake as pizza dough in my body is a very quick and easy way to gain weight.

Chapter 14 Judgement Day

Throughout the fall 2014 semester I was getting multiple head colds. This was a combination of being back in a classroom again, working in an old portable, and having students who would openly sneeze and cough in the air. It took several months of daily training, but my kids got much better at covering up when sneezing and coughing. Unfortunately, I was still getting sick.

In November, one of the teacher assistants suggested that I look into getting vitamin shots. The other benefit was that they were called slim shots and would help with weight loss as well. I scheduled a visit with the doctor's office for November 18 to begin the shots. The doctor's office was near my home in Arlington so that was a nice benefit. This is when things got ugly.

The first thing they do in the doctor's office is weigh you. I got on the scale and what I saw shocked me. I was 303.3 pounds and had gained roughly half of the weight back.

I told the nurse my story about my weight loss and she was impressed. She explained that the shot would help with increasing my metabolism. The nurse also mentioned my age, 39 at the time, and that it is much tougher to lose weight as you get older. She told me that I would need to cut out breads and starches (sweet and regular potatoes, pastas, etc.) and limit sugars.

The shot series were weekly for six weeks. After the first series of shots, I would be reevaluated and would take a three week break before starting the next series.

I realized this could not have happened at a better time. If I did not pursue getting the shots, my weight would have continued to get worse, especially with the holiday season coming up. With my annual family vacation coming up I was definitely glad to be on the shot prior to going to Las Vegas for Thanksgiving.

Upon returning from Vegas, I came to find out that I actually lost one pound that week. I was really happy considering we ate some pretty amazing food. We did a lot of walking and that combined with the shot, helped keep my weight under control.

I started to see results as December approached due to cutting out most starches. My weight loss was very slow. I lost no more than a pound per week, but I was fine with that. My main goal was to not gain weight during the holiday season. I felt so much better on the shot and did not get sick at all during November and December.

In January 2015 I was still under 300 pounds and the weight continued to come off. It was 299.3, but was still under 300. The most important fact was that I did NOT gain any weight through the holidays, which has always been an Achilles heel of mine.

I was off the shots for most of January, but started back on them in February. The biggest problem I faced was needing someone to give me the shots. I could not make it to the doctor's office in February due to coaching tennis at my school.

In late March, I was finally able to get back to the doctor's office for the weekly appointments. My tennis team won the district championship and it was time to get weighed. I was excited! I was burning a lot of calories (700-1000) per day of coaching, in addition to teaching. I felt that I would receive great news, but it was yet another lesson about weight, age, and lab tests.

Chapter 15 Science of Losing Weight

After school on March 30, I went to the doctor's office. I got on the scale and it said 297.8 pounds. It was still a weight loss, but I knew something was not right. Since 2012 I felt that something was missing. It didn't make sense to me that my weight loss was not as drastic. I felt that I should have weighed around 290. One thing I did notice was that my clothes all fit much looser, which the nurse noticed as well. However, successful and true weight loss is a combination of loose fitting clothes (inches lost) and a decrease in numbers on the dreaded scale.

The nurse suggested that I have tests done to check my thyroid and sugar levels. Getting injections was never something that bothered me, but I've always hated having blood drawn. In the past, if I saw blood I would immediately get light headed and feel faint. Regardless, I still knew something was off.

My eating habits were much better. I was eating clean again and cut out breads and potatoes. Per the nurse's advice, I was only eating apples, berries, and oranges. I cut out pineapple, bananas, and grapes. I was told to not eat those specific fruits because they were full of sugars, which would not help my weight loss. The nurse told me to give up the parfaits that I would have at school during lunch, as well as the apple sauce since both were full of sugar.

On Monday April 6, I weighed in at 296.6 so the weight was still slowly coming off due to small significant changes. I received my test results. There was good news and bad news.

The good news was that my sugar levels were great. In 2011 I was borderline type 2 diabetic with high blood sugar. That was no longer the case. Most of my tests were satisfactory because my health overall was in great shape.

There was one test that was not good. I was diagnosed with an underactive thyroid and this was why it was so difficult to lose weight. The nurse consulted with my doctor and I was put on thyroid medication called nature thyroid. It would help increase my thyroid level and would help me with my weight loss. I was also diagnosed with having a vitamin D deficiency.

I figured that I had a thyroid issue since several members of my family have this issue. The good news was that after one week I had lost three pounds with the help of the thyroid medication.

On April 13 my weight was at 292.6. The next week I was going to be in Austin, TX so I knew that my weight was going to go up a little.

I highly recommend to anyone who is planning to lose weight to get lab work done at your doctor's office. I wish I would have done this sooner. This could have saved me some frustration back in 2012 when it appeared that I had stopped losing weight.

If I would have gone to the doctor's office, I am convinced that my thyroid would have been diagnosed sooner and I would have realized that eating things like white rice was a poor decision. Maybe it would have been easier to get back on the wagon.

Addiction comes in many forms and my addiction will always be food. It is just the way my mind is wired. I know now that there are times when I don't mind putting on weight during a vacation or holiday. The key now is to realize that beforehand and make good decisions to get the weight off after that occurs.

Speaking of food, I was heading to Austin that weekend (April 18-19) for a regional initiation for DSP that my kids at UT Austin were hosting. I knew it would be a weekend of celebration as I was staying with one of my best friends and fraternity little Brother. We had several great meals that weekend including one of my biggest vices...

I love donut burgers! There, I said it! There is a great restaurant called Gourdough's in Austin, home of the world famous donut burger. I knew I would gain weight that weekend but Gourdough's was more than worth it. If I am going to gain weight, at least it will be for the best food around.

I ended up putting on a few pounds and weighed in at 295.8 on April 20, 2015. I weighed 294.4 on April 27 and 291.8 for my last weigh in on May 4, 2015.

My next series of shots resumed on June 5, and I was finally putting everything together.

Chapter 16 Forward Momentum

The school year finally ended on June 2. It was a long year, but a great year overall. I built great relationships with my kids, and we had a lot of success. We were featured on the district website multiple times for science lessons, including using a fruit salad for learning about the solar system, playing the biome habitat game to learn about biomes, and playing tennis to learn about force and motion. My tennis team won the district championship, and ended an undefeated season. They were also featured on the district website and we received UIL first place medals for winning the district championship. The standardized test results were still pending, but I was confident that my students did great in science.

I will also impart a little advice for the new and current teachers out there; Special Education is a whole different beast, and the paperwork can be a little intense. After a while, you do get more comfortable with it and I highly recommend that you consider working in Special Education because the kids are awesome.

Not everything will be perfect and there can always be challenges, especially when working in a department full of opinionated teachers and assistants. However, as a teacher, I teach for my kids. The kids and parents are what matter and as long as you focus on that, you will always have success as a teacher.

With the school year over, it was time to relax and go to the doctor's office to resume the injections. I started getting my shots on Friday mornings to give me some more time to relax during the week. Friday mornings also happened to have little to no wait in the doctor's office.

On Friday June 5, I went back to the doctor's office and received great news on my weight. I officially weighed in at 287.2 pounds. Since last November, I have lost roughly sixteen pounds and feel great.

My health is finally on track and the weight is coming off again. As I stated previously in this book, our greatest battle in life will be against ourselves. It reminds me of the old looney toons cartoons, when you would have the angel version of you on one shoulder and the devil version on your other shoulder with both whispering in your ear. You have to figure out which one to listen to because it will have a great impact on your life.

I have learned a lot of lessons about eating less and moving more over the past four years. In the next chapter I am going to specifically cover foods that I have learned to cut out, in addition to foods that I eat daily.

No eating plan is cut and dry and there will always be changes and adjustments. You will always battle cravings. I know that I have and will continue to do so.

However, there are foods that I absolutely refuse to eat, such as white rice and bread. I will also still have the occasional burger or a donut burger. In May, after volunteering at the Special Olympics, my Mom and I went to Gino's east pizza and enjoyed a Chicago deep dish that lasted us several days with leftovers. It was also only one of two times that I had pizza in six months.

Cheat meals are a good thing and should be limited because the moment you feel deprived, you will lose the battle. One of the greatest things that has happened to me is that I finally realize there are certain foods that I should not eat.

Throughout the week I enjoy foods like ribeye or London broil steaks, grilled salmon, baked cod, baked Mahi Mahi, grilled chicken, and grilled chicken leg quarters.

I will cover more of those foods in the next chapter but as you can see baked and grilled are two common themes. My foods emphasize proteins and fruits. In my next chapter I will discuss a typical week of food. This is the food I currently eat and has evolved after four years of trial and error.

I also started working out in the pool again this summer. My current workout mix for those who need a great playlist is below. My workout is currently around thirty minutes and I have gone back to just jogging and running in place for thirty minutes, but am consistently working out three days a week.

As a teacher, I have learned over the years that sometimes I just need to simplify. I want to maximize my workouts this summer, which is exactly what I have done with the current regimen I have. Thirty minutes jogging and running in place, nothing more and nothing less. Sometimes you just have to K.I.S.S. (keep it simple silly).

Brodie's Thirty Minute Workout Mix 2015

01 Rocky Theme Song

02 Rocky Training Montage

03 Turn Down for What by DJ Snake and Lil Jon

04 Phenomenal by Eminem

05 A Little Respect by Erasure

06 The Champ Is Here by Jadakiss

07 Can't Tell Me Nothing by Kayne West

08 Life Your Lift by T.I.

09 Bad Blood by Taylor Swift

This workout mix has helped me get back in the groove and is a good mix of songs, especially when potentially hitting that twenty minute wall. I am consistently in the pool three days a week for the first time in several years and I feel great.

Chapter 17 You Are What You Eat

This is a typical week of food for me. It can vary but this is usually what I eat. This is also based on being home for the summer.

Work Out Day One

Wake up

Take Thyroid Pill (have to wait thirty minutes until I can eat or drink anything)

Drink fifty ounces of water (two water bottles)

Work out

Lunch

Cobb Salad for lunch (eight ounces of grilled chicken glazed in BBQ sauce, two eggs, one third of a cucumber, four grape tomatoes, fourth of a head of lettuce, one dill pickle sliced, three slices of bacon, Kraft Italian light dressing)

French Vanilla Cappuccino (Keurig Pod, 80 calories)

Dessert or mid afternoon snack

One sliced Fuji or Gala Apple

One orange (peeled)

Drink fifty ounces of water (two water bottles)

French Vanilla Cappuccino (Keurig Pod, 80 calories)

Dinner

Grilled salmon (eight ounces) with dill sauce (lasts two meals for two people) (two dill pickles, two tablespoons pickle juice, two tablespoons of flour, half a stick of butter, half a cup of heavy whipping cream, two cups boiled water and simmer together on low heat for ten minutes) and served with Normandy frozen vegetables (from Costco) that are defrosted and steamed.

Dessert

One sliced Fuji or Gala Apple

One orange (peeled)

Strawberries (ten strawberries) and cream (heavy whipping cream, five teaspoons whipped, one equal packet)

Popsicle (tropical brand sugar free)

Drink fifty ounces of water (two water bottles)

Gelato cup (strawberry, caramel or berry flavor) (only served one or two times a week)

9 PM

Chamomile Tea (two equal packets)

One Melatonin (3 MG)

Non-Work Out Day

Wake up

Take Thyroid Pill (have to wait thirty minutes until I can eat or drink anything)

Drink fifty ounces of water (two water bottles)

French Vanilla Cappuccino (Keurig Pod, 80 calories)

Late Breakfast

Three strips of bacon, three medium eggs sunny side up, three sausage patties, and half a jalapeno cooked pepper. Food is cooked in two table spoons of olive oil.

Dessert or mid afternoon snack

One sliced Fuji or Gala Apple

One orange (peeled)

Drink fifty ounces of water (two water bottles)

French Vanilla Cappuccino (Keurig Pod, 80 calories)

Dinner

Ribeye steak (12-16 ounces) grilled medium rare and served with Normandy frozen vegetables (from Costco) that are defrosted and steamed. Steak is cooked with two tablespoons of olive oil.

Dessert

One sliced Fuji or Gala Apple

One orange (peeled)

Strawberries (ten strawberries) and cream (heavy whipping cream, five teaspoons whipped, one equal packet)

Popsicle (tropical brand sugar free)

Drink fifty ounces of water (two water bottles)

Gelato cup (strawberry, caramel or berry flavor) (only served one or two times a week)

9 PM

Chamomile Tea (two equal packets)

One Melatonin (3 MG)

Work Out Day 2

Wake up

Take Thyroid Pill (have to wait thirty minutes until I can eat or drink anything)

Drink fifty ounces of water (two water bottles)

Work out

Lunch

Cobb Salad for lunch (eight ounces of grilled chicken glazed in BBQ sauce, two eggs, one third of a cucumber, four grape tomatoes, fourth of a head of lettuce, one dill pickle sliced, three slices of bacon, Kraft Italian light dressing)

French Vanilla Cappuccino (Keurig Pod, 80 calories)

Dessert or mid afternoon snack

One sliced Fuji or Gala Apple

One orange (peeled)

Drink fifty ounces of water (two water bottles)

French Vanilla Cappuccino (Keurig Pod, 80 calories)

Dinner

Grilled chicken (twelve ounces, marinated in teriyaki sauce and BBQ sauce) and served with Normandy frozen vegetables (from Costco) that are defrosted and steamed.

Dessert

One sliced Fuji or Gala Apple

One orange (peeled)

Strawberries (ten strawberries) and cream (heavy whipping cream, five teaspoons whipped, one equal packet)

Popsicle (tropical brand sugar free)

Drink fifty ounces of water (two water bottles)

Gelato cup (strawberry, caramel or berry flavor) (only served one or two times a week)

9 PM

Chamomile Tea (two equal packets)

One Melatonin (3 MG)

Non-Work Out Day

Wake up

Take Thyroid Pill (have to wait thirty minutes until I can eat or drink anything)

Drink fifty ounces of water (two water bottles)

French Vanilla Cappuccino (Keurig Pod, 80 calories)

Late Breakfast

Three strips of bacon, three medium eggs sunny side up, three sausage patties, and half a jalapeno cooked pepper. Food is cooked in two table spoons of olive oil.

Dessert or mid afternoon snack

One sliced Fuji or Gala Apple

One orange (peeled)

Drink fifty ounces of water (two water bottles)

French Vanilla Cappuccino (Keurig Pod, 80 calories)

Dinner

Cheat Meal at restaurant (usually rotates between Razzoo's Cajun for jalapeno poppers and shrimp fondue, La Madeline for their French country breakfast, Flying Fish for their grilled fish tacos, and Spring Creek BBQ for their ribs)

Dessert

One sliced Fuji or Gala Apple

One orange (peeled)

Strawberries (ten strawberries) and cream (heavy whipping cream, five teaspoons whipped, one equal packet)

Popsicle (tropical brand sugar free)

Drink fifty ounces of water (two water bottles)

Gelato cup (strawberry, caramel or berry flavor) (only served one or two times a week)

9 PM

Chamomile Tea (two equal packets)

One Melatonin (3 MG)

Work Out Day 3

Wake up

Take Thyroid Pill (have to wait thirty minutes until I can eat or drink anything)

Drink fifty ounces of water (two water bottles)

Work out

Lunch

Cobb Salad for lunch (eight ounces of grilled chicken glazed in BBQ sauce, two eggs, one third of a cucumber, four grape tomatoes, fourth of a head of lettuce, one dill pickle sliced, three slices of bacon, Kraft Italian light dressing)

French Vanilla Cappuccino (Keurig Pod, 80 calories)

Dessert or mid afternoon snack

One sliced Fuji or Gala Apple

One orange (peeled)

Drink fifty ounces of water (two water bottles)

French Vanilla Cappuccino (Keurig Pod, 80 calories)

Dinner

Baked Cod or Mahi Mahi (ten ounces) and served with Normandy frozen vegetables (from Costco) that are defrosted and steamed.

Dessert

One sliced Fuji or Gala Apple

One orange (peeled)

Strawberries (ten strawberries) and cream (heavy whipping cream, five teaspoons whipped, one equal packet)

Popsicle (tropical brand sugar free)

Drink fifty ounces of water (two water bottles)

Gelato cup (strawberry, caramel or berry flavor) (only served one or two times a week)

9 PM

Chamomile Tea (two equal packets)

One Melatonin (3 MG)

Non-Work Out Day

Wake up

Take Thyroid Pill (have to wait thirty minutes until I can eat or drink anything)

Drink fifty ounces of water (two water bottles)

French Vanilla Cappuccino (Keurig Pod, 80 calories)

Late Breakfast

Three strips of bacon, three medium eggs sunny side up, three sausage patties, and half a jalapeno cooked pepper. Food is cooked in two table spoons of olive oil.

Dessert or mid afternoon snack

One sliced Fuji or Gala Apple

One orange (peeled)

Drink fifty ounces of water (two water bottles)

French Vanilla Cappuccino (Keurig Pod, 80 calories)

Dinner

London Broil steak (12-16 ounces) grilled medium rare and served with Normandy frozen vegetables (from Costco) that are defrosted and boiled. Steak is cooked with two tablespoons of olive oil.

Dessert

One sliced Fuji or Gala Apple

One orange (peeled)

Strawberries (ten strawberries) and cream (heavy whipping cream, five teaspoons whipped, one equal packet)

Popsicle (tropical brand sugar free)

Drink fifty ounces of water (two water bottles)

Strawberries (ten strawberries) and cream (heavy whipping cream, five teaspoons whipped, one equal packet)

Popsicle (tropical brand sugar free)

Drink fifty ounces of water (two water bottles)

Gelato cup (strawberry, caramel or berry flavor) (only served one or two times a week)

9 PM

Chamomile Tea (two equal packets)

One Melatonin (3 MG)

Non-Work Out Day

Wake up

Take Thyroid Pill (have to wait thirty minutes until I can eat or drink anything)

Drink fifty ounces of water (two water bottles)

French Vanilla Cappuccino (Keurig Pod, 80 calories)

Late Breakfast

Three strips of bacon, three medium eggs sunny side up, three sausage patties, and half a jalapeno cooked pepper. Food is cooked in two table spoons of olive oil.

Dessert or mid afternoon snack

One sliced Fuji or Gala Apple

One orange (peeled)

Drink fifty ounces of water (two water bottles)

French Vanilla Cappuccino (Keurig Pod, 80 calories)

Dinner

London Broil steak (12-16 ounces) grilled medium rare and served with Normandy frozen vegetables (from Costco) that are defrosted and boiled. Steak is cooked with two tablespoons of olive oil.

Dessert

One sliced Fuji or Gala Apple

One orange (peeled)

Strawberries (ten strawberries) and cream (heavy whipping cream, five teaspoons whipped, one equal packet)

Popsicle (tropical brand sugar free)

Drink fifty ounces of water (two water bottles)

Gelato cup (strawberry, caramel or berry flavor) (only served one or two times a week)

9 PM

Chamomile Tea (two equal packets)

One Melatonin (3 MG)

Non-Work Out Day

Wake up

Take Thyroid Pill (have to wait thirty minutes until I can eat or drink anything)

Drink fifty ounces of water (two water bottles)

French Vanilla Cappuccino (Keurig Pod, 80 calories)

Late Breakfast

Three strips of bacon, three medium eggs sunny side up, three sausage patties, and half a jalapeno cooked pepper. Food is cooked in two table spoons of olive oil.

Dessert or mid afternoon snack

One sliced Fuji or Gala Apple

One orange (peeled)

Drink fifty ounces of water (two water bottles)

French Vanilla Cappuccino (Keurig Pod, 80 calories)

Dinner

Salad (one third of a cucumber, four grape tomatoes, fourth of a head of lettuce, one dill pickle sliced, Kraft Italian light dressing)

Half a rotisserie chicken (Walmart family size) with one cup of cole slaw and Heinz 57 BBQ Sauce.

Dessert

One sliced Fuji or Gala Apple

One orange (peeled)

Strawberries (ten strawberries) and cream (heavy whipping cream, five teaspoons whipped, one equal packet)

Popsicle (tropical brand sugar free)

Drink fifty ounces of water (two water bottles)

Gelato cup (strawberry, caramel or berry flavor) (only served one or two times a week)

9 PM

Chamomile Tea (two equal packets)

One Melatonin (3 MG)

Chapter 18 Eating Clean

When I started to eat less and move more back in 2011 I noticed several things that changed. I had increased energy, slept better, rarely had an upset stomach (still get those sometimes after a cheat meal but it is rare) and felt much heathier overall.

Even when I made mistakes over the past few years, I always wanted to feel healthy. I could always tell when I was not eating right as I would feel sluggish, bloated, and would get stomach aches at night.

When I ate clean I always felt good and actually craved eating the healthier foods. I went to Las Vegas again in June for our annual family vacation. We ate very well and I did enjoy some great buffets at the Bellagio, Cosmopolitan and Aria hotel and casinos. What I did realize upon returning home through was that I missed eating clean and immediately went back to my eating routine that I have detailed in Chapter 17. I am also a huge advocate of enjoying yourself when on vacation. You can satisfy your food cravings for weeks or even months and it also reminds you how much you have missed eating right, especially after a five day vacation of eating foods that you would not typically eat when eating clean.

Eating clean does become part of your lifestyle over time and over the past four years I always had to eat fruit at least once a day. Strawberries (in season), apples, and grapes were my favorites. On the advice of my nurse I have cut out grapes but still eat strawberries, apples, and oranges. I avoid bananas, melons, and especially pineapples.

I have also noticed on multiple occasions the improvement in how I feel when I cut out breads. White bread was always avoided unless I was eating out but I did eat whole grain bread at home. I used to eat whole grain bread but stopped eating that bread last November. Once I gave up all breads (with the exception of the occasional cheat meal at a restaurant) I felt much better and rarely felt bloated as bread always seemed to have that effect on me.

Water also had a huge effect in on how I felt. Typically, when most people wake up, they can potentially be dehydrated or close to it. To start each day, I always drink fifty ounces of water. I have four water bottles that each hold twenty five ounces in each bottle.

Water is a huge benefit in my view, especially when you start your day. It helps me feel refreshed. You will increase your bathroom visits in a day, but all of that water helps your body, kidneys and other internal organs.

Another key thing that will help you get through the day is snacks. It will help with keeping your energy up throughout the day. The next chapter will show my food plan when I am teaching and you will see that I snack often.

Chapter 19 Eating Habits during the School Year

The following is a typical five day work week eating plan that I have. At the start of the school year I had way too many snacks that were not healthy enough. The foods I ate at the start of the school year included potato chips, yogurt parfaits, apple sauce, teddy graham snack packs, and multiple individual fruit Mentos (Aldi brand). It took a while to create a proper eating plan for the week and by March the schedule below was what I typically ate throughout the week. I threw out the snacks that I should not have been eating in my classroom and stopped getting the parfaits and applesauce in the cafeteria during lunch.

Monday

Wake up at 6:00 am

Take Thyroid Pill (have to wait thirty minutes until I can eat or drink anything)

Drink fifty ounces of water (two water bottles)

French Vanilla Cappuccino (Keurig Pod, 80 calories)

Arrive at school

Second French Cappuccino (Kuerig Pod, 80 calories) (I have a second Kuerig machine in my classroom)

Mid-Morning Snack

Protein Meal Bar Double Chocolate (Fit and Active Brand from Aldi, 190 calories)

Lunch

Four small turkey rolls (Costco), one serving of uncooked broccoli, one serving of grape tomatoes, one serving of cucumbers, two small ranch dressing cups, one granny smith apple and one small orange

Twenty five ounces of water (one water bottle)

Conference Period Workout (students are at gym for PE)

Play tennis with my kids for 15-20 minutes

Afternoon snack

One apple

Twenty five ounces of water (one water bottle)

Dinner

London Broil steak (12-16 ounces) grilled medium rare and served with Normandy frozen vegetables (from Costco) that are defrosted and steamed. Steak is cooked with two tablespoons of olive oil.

Dessert

One sliced Fuji or Gala Apple

One orange (peeled)

Strawberries (ten strawberries) and cream (heavy whipping cream, five teaspoons whipped, one equal packet)

Popsicle (tropical brand sugar free)

Drink fifty ounces of water (two water bottles)

Gelato cup (strawberry, caramel or berry flavor) (only served one or two times a week)

9 PM

Chamomile Tea (two equal packets)

One Melatonin (3 MG)

Tuesday

Wake up at 6:00 am

Take Thyroid Pill (have to wait thirty minutes until I can eat or drink anything)

Drink fifty ounces of water (two water bottles)

French Vanilla Cappuccino (Keurig Pod, 80 calories)

Arrive at school

Second French Cappuccino (Kuerig Pod, 80 calories)

Mid-Morning Snack

Protein Meal Bar Double Chocolate (Fit and Active Brand from Aldi, 190 calories)

Lunch

Buffalo Chicken Wrap from Cafeteria (school has a healthy food section), one serving of uncooked broccoli, one serving of grape tomatoes, one serving of cucumbers, two small ranch dressing cups, one granny smith apple and one small orange

Twenty five ounces of water (one water bottle)

Conference Period Workout (students are at gym for PE)

Play tennis with my kids for 15-20 minutes

Afternoon snack

One granny smith apple

Twenty five ounces of water (one water bottle)

Dinner

Baked Cod or Mahi Mahi (ten ounces) and served
with Normandy frozen vegetables (from Costco)
that are defrosted and steamed.

Dessert

One sliced Fuji or Gala Apple

One orange (peeled)

Strawberries (ten strawberries) and cream (heavy
whipping cream, five teaspoons whipped, one
equal packet)

Popsicle (tropical brand sugar free)

Drink fifty ounces of water (two water bottles)

Gelato cup (strawberry, caramel or berry flavor)
(only served one or two times a week)

9 PM

Chamomile Tea (two equal packets)

One Melatonin (3 MG)

Wednesday

Wake up at 6:00 am

Take Thyroid Pill (have to wait thirty minutes until I can eat or drink anything)

Drink fifty ounces of water (two water bottles)

French Vanilla Cappuccino (Keurig Pod, 80 calories)

Arrive at school

Second French Cappuccino (Kuerig Pod, 80 calories)

Mid-Morning Snack

Protein Meal Bar Double Chocolate (Fit and Active Brand from Aldi, 190 calories)

Lunch

Four small turkey rolls (Costco), one serving of uncooked broccoli, one serving of grape tomatoes, one serving of cucumbers, two small ranch dressing cups, one granny smith apple and one small orange

Twenty five ounces of water (one water bottle)

Conference Period Workout (students are at gym for PE)

Play tennis with my kids for 15-20 minutes

Afternoon snack

One apple

Twenty five ounces of water (one water bottle)

Dinner

Cheat Meal at restaurant (usually rotates between Razzoo's Cajun for jalapeno poppers and shrimp fondue, La Madeline for their French country breakfast, Flying Fish for their grilled fish tacos, and Spring Creek BBQ for their ribs)

Dessert

One sliced Fuji or Gala Apple

One orange (peeled)

Strawberries (ten strawberries) and cream (heavy whipping cream, five teaspoons whipped, one equal packet)

Popsicle (tropical brand sugar free)

Drink fifty ounces of water (two water bottles)

Gelato cup (strawberry, caramel or berry flavor) (only served one or two times a week)

9 PM

Chamomile Tea (two equal packets)

One Melatonin (3 MG)

Thursday

Wake up at 6:00 am

Take Thyroid Pill (have to wait thirty minutes until I can eat or drink anything)

Drink fifty ounces of water (two water bottles)

French Vanilla Cappuccino (Keurig Pod, 80 calories)

Arrive at school

Second French Cappuccino (Kuerig Pod, 80 calories)

Mid-Morning Snack

Protein Meal Bar Double Chocolate (Fit and Active Brand from Aldi, 190 calories)

Lunch

Buffalo Chicken Wrap from Cafeteria (school has a healthy food section), one serving of uncooked broccoli, one serving of grape tomatoes, one serving of cucumbers, two small ranch dressing cups, one granny smith apple and one small orange

Twenty five ounces of water (one water bottle)

Conference Period Workout (students are at gym for PE)

Play tennis with my kids for 15-20 minutes

Afternoon snack

One granny smith apple

Twenty five ounces of water (one water bottle)

Dinner

Half a rotisserie chicken (Walmart family size) with one cup of cole slaw and Heinz 57 BBQ Sauce.

Dessert

One sliced Fuji or Gala Apple

One orange (peeled)

Strawberries (ten strawberries) and cream (heavy whipping cream, five teaspoons whipped, one equal packet)

Popsicle (tropical brand sugar free)

Drink fifty ounces of water (two water bottles)

Gelato cup (strawberry, caramel or berry flavor) (only served one or two times a week)

9 PM

Chamomile Tea (two equal packets)

One Melatonin (3 MG)

Friday

Wake up at 6:00 am

Take Thyroid Pill (have to wait thirty minutes until I can eat or drink anything)

Drink fifty ounces of water (two water bottles)

French Vanilla Cappuccino (Keurig Pod, 80 calories)

Arrive at school

Second French Cappuccino (Kuerig Pod, 80 calories)

Mid-Morning Snack

Protein Meal Bar Double Chocolate (Fit and Active Brand from Aldi, 190 calories)

Lunch

Four small turkey rolls (Costco), one serving of uncooked broccoli, one serving of grape tomatoes, one serving of cucumbers, two small ranch dressing cups, one granny smith apple and one small orange

Twenty five ounces of water (one water bottle)

Conference Period Workout (students are at gym for PE)

Play tennis with my kids for 15-20 minutes

Afternoon snack

One apple

Twenty five ounces of water (one water bottle)

Dinner

Grilled chicken (twelve ounces, marinated in teriyaki sauce and BBQ sauce) and served with

Normandy frozen vegetables (from Costco) that are defrosted and steamed.

Dessert

One sliced Fuji or Gala Apple

One orange (peeled)

Strawberries (ten strawberries) and cream (heavy whipping cream, five teaspoons whipped, one equal packet)

Popsicle (tropical brand sugar free)

Drink fifty ounces of water (two water bottles)

Gelato cup (strawberry, caramel or berry flavor) (only served one or two times a week)

9 PM

Chamomile Tea (two equal packets)

One Melatonin (3 MG)

Chapter 20 Changing Your Lifestyle

One thing I want to make clear is that changing your lifestyle is not easy. I wanted to cover both the success and challenges that I have had throughout this book in order to show the struggle. There are several virtual guarantees that I can make should you choose to want to make lifestyle changes in your own life.

First things first, you will take your eye off the ball at some point. You will go back to bad eating. I love movies, especially the Rocky movies (with the exception of Rocky V) and the Dark Knight Trilogy. In Rocky Balboa, Rocky gave some advice to his son about how life will knock you down. *Rocky told his son that life was not about how hard you hit, but it was about how hard you can get hit and keep moving forward.* Changing your lifestyle is the same thing.

When you lose sight of your goal, what will you do? Will you move forward or will you lie down and go back to your old ways? There were times when I just laid on the ground and took the hits. After losing over sixty-seven pounds I took those hits. I let my weight increase and did not care for a while. Naturally, my weight increased again, but I figured that I lost so much weight it didn't matter.

Last summer I went back to eating clean and working out, but I did not weigh myself. I could see the improvement in the mirror and clothes fit better, still I didn't hold myself accountable. My stomach felt smaller, yet I didn't know for sure.

What I have realized is that weighing yourself MUST be a part of the process. It is the only way to truly know whether you are losing the weight. There is nothing better than seeing your clothes fit loosely, but the true accountability is seeing the numbers drop on the scale.

When I had that early June weigh in showing the sixteen pound weight loss, it felt like a huge victory. Not only were my clothes fitting looser, but my weight showed real progress. The nurse mentioned that out of all of the patients on the slim shot, my weight loss was the second highest. That was a great feeling.

One of the main themes in The Dark Knight trilogy is why do we fall? We fall so that we can get back up. We can choose to rise and become the person we know that we can be. Choose to RISE. I actually created an acronym for RISE in my Positivity Attracts seminar. R was for Resilient, I was for Inspire, S was for Selfless, and E was for Energy. I believe that if you have all four parts of the acronym then you have made the decision to rise and get back up. Dust yourself off and move forward.

Our greatest opponent is in the mirror. The greatest battle in life is not against another person, it is against ourselves. In life, the only perception that truly matters, is what we think of our own life. It doesn't matter what someone else thinks of you.

Chapter 21 Turning Forty

On June 10, 2015 I officially turned the big 40. I had an amazing birthday. Several days later I had an epic birthday party with many of my closest friends from DSP, education, and people who I have worked with over the last twenty plus years. It reminded me what really matters in life. Family and friends. My grandfather gave me a lot of great advice in my youth, but one piece of advice in particular always stayed with me. My pappas (my nickname for my grandfather) told me that *it was never how old you are, but how old you feel both mentally and physically.*

When I officially turned forty I didn't feel any different. Turning the big 40 quite honestly terrified me. I started to worry that maybe I would have a mid-life crisis like my father did (I shall save those stories for a future book), or that I would start to get old and not be the same person I was. None of that happened.

I did want to do something epic, so I decided to get two tattoos. After much consideration, I decided that I would get a star tattoo on my upper left arm and a treble clef tattoo on my upper right arm. Two good friends of mine who were also teachers went with me to get the tattoos done.

After roughly four hours, I had both tattoos done and they looked great.

My single act of rebellion to commemorate my 40th birthday was done and I loved both of the tattoos and the symbolic nature behind them. The star signifies the lone star of Texas being blue and gold, as well as the alumni chapter that I was a founder of (Arlington Area Lone Star Alumni) and the Dallas Cowboys (my all-time favorite sports team). The treble clef was the same shade of blue with white in the tattoo. It signifies my love of music. Music is one of my prime motivators in life. The treble clef represents my love of singing both in school at Bowie and UT Arlington, as well as on a professional level with Schola Cantorum of Texas.

The one thing that I was most proud of was that I made it to forty. I honestly feel that if I would not have changed my lifestyle and chosen to RISE, then I would not be where I am today. Roughly four years ago I was 336 pounds, borderline type 2 diabetic, and recently recovered from both bronchitis and pneumonia. If I would have continued on that path, I am convinced that I would not be here today.

I have made mistakes on this journey, but I took hits, and finally got back up. In doing so, I chose to rise and move forward.

I want to thank my friends and family who have supported me in this journey. It is far from over and the battles in life will continue. My goal was always to get to 250 pounds. I was close once and I will be close again. My weight loss is going to be slower and it will have challenges. Whether it takes one year or ten years, I WILL hit that 250 pound goal.

I know I'll fall down, but I'm only human. Hopefully my experiences will help in your journey. My life goal is to always to have the power of one. With this book I vow to help at least one person. I hope that person is you.

About the Author

Paul Brodie is the President of BrodieEDU, an education consulting firm that specializes in the development of literacy programs, motivational seminars for universities and corporations, and wellness education. Brodie also serves as a Special Education Teacher for the Hurst-Euless-Bedford Independent School District.

From 2011-2014, Brodie served as a Grant Coordinator for the ASPIRE program in the

Birdville Independent School District. As coordinator, he created instructional and enrichment programming for over 800 students and 100 parents in the ASPIRE before and after school programs. He also served for many years on the Board of Directors for the Leadership Development Council, Inc with leading the implementation of educational programming in low cost housing.

Previously, Brodie spent many years in the corporate world and decided to leave a lucrative career in the medical field to follow his passion and transitioned into education. From 2008 to 2011, he was a highly successful teacher in Arlington, TX where he taught English as a Second Language. Brodie turned a once struggling ESL program into one of the top programs in the school district. Many of his students have moved on to journalism, AVID, art classes, and a number of the students exited the ESL program entirely. His methods included music, movies, graphic novels, and many high engagement methods including using technology, games, cultural celebrations, and getting parents involved in their children's education. Brodie's approach has been called unconventional but highly effective, revolutionary, and highly engaging.

Brodie earned an M.A. in Teaching from Louisiana College and B.B.A. in Management from the University of Texas at Arlington. He recently completed his first book: Eat Less and Move More: My Journey. Brodie hopes the book will help those like himself that have had challenges with weight and the goal of the book is to promote not only weight loss but also health and wellness.

His motivational seminars have been featured at multiple universities and at leadership conferences across the United States since 2005. Brodie is active in professional organizations and within the community and currently serves on the Advisory Board for Advent Urban Youth Development and as a volunteer with the Special Olympics. He continues to be involved with The International Business Fraternity of Delta Sigma Pi and has served in many positions since 2002 including National Vice President – Organizational Development, Leadership Foundation Trustee, National Organizational Development Chair, District Director, and in many other volunteer leadership roles. He resides in Arlington, TX.

Acknowledgments

Thank you to God for guidance and protection throughout my life.

Thank YOU the reader for investing your time reading this book.

Thank you to my amazing mom, Barbara Brodie for all of the years of support and a kick in the butt when needed.

Thank you to my awesome sister, Dr. Heather Ottaway for the help and feedback with not only my book but also with my motivational seminars. It is scary how similar we are.

Thank you to Devin Hacker for serving as the editor of this book. The slicing and dicing was very much appreciated and I could not have gotten this book published without her assistance.

Thank you to Lindsay Palmer who is working tirelessly to get me booked on college campuses for seminars throughout the United States. I could not have a better team of people to work with on Team Brodie.

Thank you to all who have served on the BrodieEDU Advisory Board.

Thank you to my dad, Bill "The Wild Scotsman" Brodie for his encouragement and support with the startup process of this book.

Thank you to Shannon and Robert Winckel (two members of the four horsemen with myself and our good friend, Derrada Rubell-Asbell) for their friendship and support. Shannon and Robert are two of my best teacher friends and are always great sounding boards for ideas.

Thank you to (Don) Omar Sandoval for his friendship and help with several BrodieEDU projects including building our awesome website.

Thank you to Tyler Wagner for writing my foreword and for his assistance with publishing this book.

Thank you to all of the amazing friends that I have worked with over the past twenty plus years. Each of them has made a great impact on my life.

Thank you to all of my students that I have had the honor to teach over the years. I am very proud of each of my kids.

Thank you to Delta Sigma Pi Business Fraternity. I learned a great deal about public speaking and leadership through the organization and every experience that I have had helped me become the person that I am today.

Thank you to my three best friends: J. Dean Craig, Jen Moorman, and Aaron Krzycki. We have gone through a lot together and I look forward to many more years of friendship.

Thank you to all of the students past and present at the UT Arlington and UT Austin chapters of DSP. Both schools mean a lot to me and I look forward to seeing them again at some point in the near future.

Thank you to the Lott Family (Stacy, Kerry, Lexi, and Austin) for their friendship over the past six years.

Thank you to Robin Clites for always taking care of things at the house with ensuring that Mom and I can always get that family vacation every year.

Contact Information

Interested in booking Paul for seminars, coaching, or consulting?

Paul can be reached at Brodie@BrodieEDU.com

Website http://www.BrodieEDU.com

@BrodieEDU on Twitter

BrodieEDU Facebook Page

BrodieEDU YouTube Channel

Feedback

Please leave a review for my book as I would greatly appreciate your feedback.

I also welcome you to contact me with any suggestions at Brodie@BrodieEDU.com